Ultimate MILF
10 XXX
Porn Star Interviews

Avelina Fleur

Avelina Fleur

ISBN: 9781549908194

Dedication

ML...

FEATURED PORN STARS

Ultimate MILF:

10 XXX Porn Star Interviews

Possessing an insatiable compulsion for sex, I've had the esteemed privilege, honor, and thrill of befriending and interviewing the world's most beautiful and sexually empowered porn stars. Through valued friendships, intimate moments of hardcore revelation, and naughty girl talk, it's my honor to offer you candid interviews from porn's *Ultimate MILFS*. Without further ado, I proudly give you porn's hottest mamas..

Aaliyah Love

Birth Date: June 11

Hometown: Chicago, IL

Height: 5'2"

Weight: 109 lbs.

Measurements: 33B-25-34

Movies:

Virtual Date with Aaliyah Love- Amateur Teen Kingdom

Aaliyah Love's Female Obsession- Vivid

Aaliyah Love Experience- Girlfriends Films

Aaliyah Love 1- Naughty America

Aaliyah Love- AE Films

After doing a bit of research on you, we discovered that you were a preschool teacher before porn. Did you hold other jobs aside from that one?

AL: Yes, I was a preschool teacher. I also attended college to get my degree in education, and am more than half way there. I never in a million years thought that I would end up in porn. It's kind of crazy.

So your next step was from preschool teacher to web-cam model, correct?

AL: Basically, it's a shame that I can get paid 3X's as much to take my clothes off as I can teaching our nation's children. Bottom line, I was really broke, only making between forty to fifty dollars per day. At one point, I was only a few steps away from being homeless. I used my college loans to help pay my bills. It's then when I discovered web-camming. My thought process was that when I was done teaching for the day, I would go to the studio and work for an hour or two in order to catch up on my bills.

It sounds as though web-camming was only intended to be a short-term plan.

AL: Yes, I thought I'd do it for three or four months, save the money I earned, and finally get ahead of my bills. That was twelve years ago!

When you finally got your beak wet in web-camming, so to speak, what did your shows consist of?

AL: I started out doing solo masturbation work to begin with. That was what I was comfortable with for the first year or so. There was a lot of masturbating, talking, body play. You'd be surprised how many guys don't want to watch me masturbate but would rather just talk with me instead. Other people had more obscure requests, like putting on a pair of pink socks and jumping on a bed.

Since you had never done anything like that before, were you nervous?

AL: Yes, at that point I had never even used a dildo on myself before. I couldn't even say the word or touch it. On my first day, a dildo was given to me.

I said, "Oh no! I can't do that!"

They asked me, "What did you expect to do today?"

I replied, "I'm not sure, but certainly not that!"

So the first day continued and I was asked to stick the dildo in my butt. It was then when I stepped back and realized what my new job was really all about. (laughing)

So, it sounds like you were very naive and inexperienced when it came to sex and sexual expression, at that point.

AL: Absolutely. I was shy. I was a prude. And, even though many women don't like to admit this aloud, I wasn't very happy with my body. I thought I needed big boobs to be desirable and beautiful. It never occurred to me that there are many ways for a woman to be beautiful. While web-camming, I begin seeing myself in a different light. I started seeing my body in a different way. I was sexy too. Porn has done nothing but give me self-confidence where I had none before. It makes me feel good about myself. Everything that I've discovered I like sexually has been because of porn. It has changed my life for the better.

It sounds as though porn has been a major accomplishment in your life.

AL: Yes, it really has. I'll read a script and see what I am to do that day. I'll say, "Okay, I'll give this a try." I'll either like it or I won't, but I will try it with an open mind and see how I feel about it afterwards. Usually, I find that I am really into most stuff after I've tried it out. Porn has taught me so much about my body. It has introduced me to things I never would have tried out sexually had it not been for porn.

So then, what is an example of one sexual act that you weren't so sure about but ended up loving after giving it a go?

AL: Threesomes! I just started doing boy/girl a year ago and that has been awesome. Sometime last year, I performed in my first threesome and got to pick out the talent myself. Since I'm perpetually single, I've always been invited into threesomes but had never done it up until that point. Now, threesome are my favorite. I'm always trying to book myself for threesomes. It's really the best of both worlds.

For your first threesome, who were the lucky girl and guy?

AL: The girl was Cherie DeVille and the guy was Danny Mountain. Both of those people are so hot. He's the type of guy that girls want to climb on top of.

So, back then, what made you decide to go from solo to girl/girl, which is a feat in itself?

AL: Honestly, it was a financial decision. I realized I could make twice as much if I begin working with women. My first time with a girl was on the web-cam. She was a girl that I knew, who actually worked in the studio right next to me. After we had sex, I told her she was my first girl and she said, "Oh no, why didn't you tell me." I told her that I didn't want her to know how nervous I really was.

How did your first lesbian scene go?

AL: I loved it. I really loved it. I loved it so much that I'm still having sex with lots of girls to this day.

When going down on this girl, what technique did you implement? Did you simply do to her what men had done to you?

AL: I think I would have had a much better first time experience had it not been for web-camming. It would have been better in my private life or in a movie scene. With web-camming, there are lots of stops and starts, depending on what your viewer wants you to do or what they want to see. They purchase minutes and want to get their end result very quickly. Once they've clicked out, you cover up and wait for the next show to begin and start all over again. It usually happens in ten-minute increments. It was more like putting on a sex show rather than having actual sex. We did enjoy it, but it wasn't like we got to take our time, kiss, do some foreplay, have some sex, and so forth. It's hard to build passion with so many stops and starts. At least in porn scenes, you have long stretches of uninterrupted time to enjoy your partner.

What is your pussy eating technique?

AL: I never knew if I was good as eating pussy or not. After eating so many at this point and getting loads of feedback, it turns out that I'm very good at eating pussy. Women tell me that I'm awesome at it. I'm kind of rough with my tongue. I pay lots of attention to the clit and don't use my fingers most times. I press my tongue really hard against their clit and go up and down, trying to keep a steady momentum. I don't know if I'd recommend my style to others because my tongue gets really tired. (laughing)

Can you offer some good pussy eating advice?

AL: There is not one way to eat a pussy. Every girl and every pussy is different. Sometimes even my technique is not enjoyable for some women. It may be too much pressure or too overwhelming for them. What I can tell you is that all women will do everything they can to let you know what they like and don't like. All you have to do is pick-up on the clues. If she's moaning and bucking her hips, continue doing what you are doing. If she's trying to push you away with her hands, you may want to change things up. Repetitive motion is the key to oral sex.

Do you implement that same type of technique when you are sucking cock?

AL: Well, on camera, especially if the man is showing off, he is fucking your mouth instead of you sucking his dick, if you know what I mean. Men in porn like to fuck your face. My only technique in that scenario is not to puke. (laughing) I don't suck really hard. I try to use my mouth, my tongue, and my hands. I keep things wet and use good eye contact. I think men are much easier to please then women. So long as their cock is in your mouth, they're going to enjoy it.

So then, after deciding to add women onto your repertoire, when did you decide to also include men?

AL: At first, I was such a stickler when saying that I would NEVER do boys on camera.

Web fans would say, "Yeah, that's what they all say! It's only a matter of time."

I would get so angry with them and say, "You don't know me. You don't know my body. No I won't. You couldn't be more wrong!"

Less than a year later, I was screwing guys on camera (laughing) Once again, porn has taught me to never say never.

Since you were so steadfast on your stance of not doing boy/girl, what made you change your mind?

AL: When I was at the AVN Award show in Las Vegas a few years ago, I was hanging out with my friends, who were boy/girl performers, and thought to myself, "Are these people somehow having more fun than what I am having?" I finally realized that I was missing out big time. I thought at that moment, if I don't do this now I'm always going to regret and wonder what it would have been like. So, I tried it out.

Do you have any regrets about your decision now?

AL: Yes. My only regret is that I didn't choose to do boy/girl sooner.

It's never too late to make up for lost time.

AL: I'm doing a really job of that right now.

Since adding more protein to your diet, who have been some of your favorite male performers to work with?

AL: Johnny Sins, Johnny Castle, Ryan Driller, Erik Everhard, Steven St. Croix. As you can see, I have many favorites. I'm a very lucky girl.

We saw you do a hot scene with Bill Bailey in *Star Kissed*- Wicked Pictures.

AL: That was my first feature. I did one scene with Tyler Nixon and another with Bill Bailey. Both scenes were hot.

What was it like working on your first feature, in the lead role?

AL: When I first started doing boy/girl, I had signed an exclusive deal with MindGeek to shoot seven scenes. I began shooting *Star Kissed* the very next day after my contract was up. I couldn't believe my luck. I was working for Wicked Pictures, in the starring role of a feature film. I could have pinched myself. I had never acted before. It was amazing. It was so much fun for me. I had to memorize lines and act out a part in a different way. I hope my fans enjoyed the show.

But, prior to your lead role in *Star Kissed*, weren't you ever cast in any lesbian features that required you to learn scripts?

AL: Sure, I did a few movies for Filly Films. To compare, my Filly Films script wouldn't be more that a few pages of dialogue and we'd shoot it in a few hours. Whereas *Star Kissed* had thirty-five pages of script and took a series of days to shoot.

Was it difficult to learn all of those lines?

AL: Let me begin by saying that I am addicted to Twitter. So, whenever I would have the urge to go on Twitter, I would reach for my script instead. Repetition made it all sink in.

Are you a size queen?

AL: No, not at all. It's not really about size. Inside of porn, there is such a thing as being too big. Outside of porn, there isn't such a thing as being too small. I've never looked at a dick and rejected it based on size. It's about chemistry. It's about the chemistry between two people. It's the way he makes me feel, the way he kisses me, the way he fucks me. Thankfully, I cum really hard, fast, and easy. No matter what, I'm going to cum really hard and fast and often. I've even had directors tell me to tone down the fake orgasms. I'm like, "Who's faking! I just come a lot. This is all real. And you should be happy."

So then, who in porn has the type of cock that you can't get enough of?

AL: Before porn, I was always anti-foreskin and I don't know why. It's ridiculous. I don't even know if I was ever even with someone with foreskin before porn. I was prejudice against the foreskin. Now, I love foreskin. If a man has foreskin, I'm guaranteed to have more orgasms. I don't know why that is. I haven't figured out the science of that, and don't think I want to. All I know is that now I love men with foreskin. Mr. Pete, Mick Blue, most of the foreign guys all have great foreskin. I guess the extra skin just gives me more slip 'n slide.

Are there some male performers that you are not interested in working with because they are too large?

AL: I'm not really afraid of the big dick guys. At first, I am a bit nervous, but I really get into it. Once I start fucking them, then everything is okay. With a larger dick guy, you are going to get much sorer, much faster. With medium dick guys, you can fuck all day.

Have you ever thought about performing in interracial scenes, with our extra-large black stallions?

AL: Like I said before, I will revert back to my old line of... never say never. We'll see what happens.

****

Briana Banks

Birth Date: May 21

Hometown: Germany

Height: 5'11"

Weight: 125 lbs.

Measurements: 34DD-27-35

Movies:

And the Winner is... Briana Banks- Vivid

Briana Banks- Legend

Briana Banks Cockstar- JM Productions

Briana Banks is Busty and Lusty- Airerose Entertainment

The Best of Briana Banks 2- Coast to Coast

Can you tell us details from one of the hottest scenes you've ever been in so far?

BB: It's a toss up between a scene I did with Bobby Vitale in *Too Nasty to Tame*, shot at the famous light house. That scene was so hardcore, nasty, and raw. To this day it's still my favorite scene to watch. And, there's also a scene from the movie *Heart Breaker* where Evan Stone and I actually break the couch we're working on. Without fail, Evan Stone and I always seem to break furniture with our aggressive fucking. I love working with him.

If you weren't doing porn, what would be your fantasy job?

BB: I would love to be a supermodel and strut myself down a runway. It also would have been great to be a newscaster. I guess deep down inside I've always wanted to be in front of the public. What can I say, I'm a born entertainer.

Is it easy to make you cum? What's the best way to get you off?

BB: It's so easy to make me cum if I'm really into the person I'm with. All they have to do is stay on my clit with their fingers and mouth and I'll explode. I'm huge on clitoral stimulation. Huge!

What's your favorite position? Why?

BB: I love being fucked doggie style while looking at a mirror. I love the titillation of watching and feeling myself being fucked at the same time. Balls slapping against my ass also turns me on. I love seeing his face while he fucks me.

What turns you on?

BB: A better question is what doesn't turn me on? (laughing) What turns me on the most is knowing that the person I'm with is turned on by me. I need to feel the chemistry and see passion in their eyes. Sensual kissing also turns me on. If I kiss someone and there is nothing behind it, I'm instantly turned off. A bad kisser generally means they'll be horrible in bed. This is a rule that hasn't failed yet in my experience.

What turns you off?

BB: Aside from bad kissing, people who are not hygienic turn me off. Also, people who rush through the foreplay and are anxious to only satiate their individual needs turn me off. I love foreplay and want to be properly explored and played with before I'm fucked. Lazy people need not apply.

What are you best at sexually?

BB: I'm known for my blowjobs because I have no gag reflex. I didn't realize this talent before porn because the guys I had been with didn't have porno-sized cocks. I'm able to relax my throat muscles completely and ingest any cock. I can go all the way down to the balls with zero problems. Just bring 'em on.

What's the best way to suck cock?

BB: I love to start off slow and tease the cock. I like to suck and lick around the balls and shaft, getting it nice and wet. I want to make the guy crazy for my mouth. I'll slowly inch my way down until he's completely down my neck. I'm also a big spitter. I like things wet!

What's the best way to suck pussy?

BB: I love to suck pussy the same way, with lots of spit and pressure on the clit. I also do this flip thing with my tongue (demonstrating) that girls seem to like. I thoroughly enjoy pussy eating and perfecting my technique. I love the way they taste and feel across my tongue. I definitely have fun with it. A good rule to follow is, if you really don't enjoy sucking pussy then don't!

Describe the perfect pussy. Who in the industry has such a pussy?

BB: There isn't such a thing as the 'perfect pussy' in my opinion. Every pussy is unique and has its own personality. I enjoy all of them. I personally have a puffy pussy but am welcoming to any and all that want to play.

Do you like to masturbate? Tell us how?

BB: Oh God yes! I love to fuck myself. The best thing ever invented was the Pocket Rocket and the Temptress. Those are my favorites and the only toys I have in my drawer. If I'm horny all it takes is two to five minutes of holding the Pocket Rocket to my clit before I explode. I just make sure to have fresh batteries on hand at all time and I'm good to go.

Do you have a particular masturbation fantasy?

BB: I try to quiet my mind of all thought and instead focus all of my attention on my clit, really getting into the sensation of the buzzing riding through my pussy. That feeling is amazing. Sometimes if there is the scent of my guy's cologne on the pillow I'll masturbate to his smell and fantasize about him fucking me.

Had you been with girls in your private life before becoming a porn star?

BB: Never! I was so scared the first time I was ever with a girl that I thought I was going to pee myself. I was so intimidated by her and her big boobies. I remember the scene perfectly. It was with Lida Chase and TT Boy. She guided me though the entire process. Thank god she was very nice to me. Needless to say my pussy licking skills sucked that day. I had no idea how to eat a pussy, so Lida did all of the work. I think I've made up for it though, don't you? (laughing)

Where is the oddest place you've ever had sex?

BB: It was hanging off the edge of a high rise building in Los Angeles at 3 o'clock in the morning with Mark Davis. It was a hot scene but I was so damn cold. People were honking as they drove by because huge spotlights were on us. I also fucked on a rock with the ocean tide all around us. Not the most comfortable experiences but definitely the most memorable.

What makes you unique?

BB: My fans have really had the opportunity to see me grow both professionally and sexually before their eyes. My first girl on girl experience was in front of the camera. I had hardly any prior knowledge about sex before joining the industry. I had never been in the 69 position or had my pussy eaten out for that matter. All of my sexual growth has been captured by the camera. That makes me sexually unique, wouldn't you say?

Who are your all time favorite performers to work with? Why?

BB: I would have to choose Evan Stone, because we have amazing chemistry, Jenna Jameson for the same reason and because we can't keep our hands off each other and Joel Lawrence. I wish he were still performing. I've always enjoyed his personality and good sense of humor. He was always a pleasure.

Are you quiet or noisy during sex?

BB: Oh girl I am loud! I couldn't keep quiet even if I tried my absolute best. I'm just not a quiet person. If I'm excited you are going to know it.

Who would you invite to the perfect orgy?

BB: Angelina Jolie, Wentworth Miller, Gisele Bundchen, Johnny Depp, and Joaquin Phoenix. I'm trying to imagine all of those combined bodies. Damn, that would be a good time. That line-up is perfect!

What do you think is your best feature?

BB: My eyes. They are very expressive and I've been told they are beautiful.

What is the most sensitive part of your body?

BB: I would have to say the back of my neck, around my ears, and down my shoulder are the most sensitive. I can't forget about my clit. That part of me is extremely sensitive as are my nipples. They turn hard and pointy like erasers once I'm turned on. I'd also like to add that I absolutely hate for my feet to be touched. That is one of my biggest turn offs. Besides, there are better parts of my body to play with.

Does size matter? How do you prefer your cocks?

BB: Of course size matters. I'm not going to lie. There is such a thing as being too big and being too small. I love cocks that are in between. I have a pretty small torso, but I have to admit I did take Rocco Siffredi and another guy in a DP. Those guys are not human though. I'll just say that eight inches is great, coupled with solid girth is heaven.

Are you wilder on or off screen?

BB: It depends on who I'm with. I've had some pretty crazy sex with porno guys off screen and on. I usually scare regular guys. I have to take it down a notch for the 'civilians'.

Is there anyone you'd like to work with that you haven't yet?

BB: I'm happy to admit I've worked with almost everyone. That's very exciting to be able to say that and have it be the truth. However, I never got the opportunity to work with Janine or Jesse Jane. We would undoubtedly tear each other up. Maybe one day.

****

Cherie Deville

Birth Date: August 30

Hometown: Washington D.C.

Height: 5'5"

Weight: 110 lbs

Measurements: 32DD-23-36

Movies:

Cherie DeVille Experience- Girlfriends Films

No Limits Cherie DeVille- Zero Tolerance

Cherie- Elegant Angel

Art of Anal Sex- Tushy.com

The Sexual Desire of Cherie DeVille- New Sensations

We understand that you're just getting back home from a shoot with Kink.com. Do you shoot BDSM material often?

CD: I shoot with them once or twice a month, so, yes, rather often. I love working for Kink. It's always a great time. On this particular shoot, I got to dabble with electricity play. I worked with Aiden Starr, who is an awesomely talented and sexy performer. We had an electrifying time together. (laughing)

Cherie, you are such a dichotomy. Outwardly, you look like a girl-next-door, collegiate type of woman, but inside you are a sexual deviant! Have you surprised your lovers with this unexpected dichotomy?

CD: Yes, I have surprised a few! I should have a resume that I pass out beforehand. My look is very wholesome and I do tend to dress more conservatively. That just happens to be the type of presentation and clothing style that I prefer. Compared to most people, I do tend to enjoy the more unusual aspects of sex.

So you're the proverbial she-wolf in sheep's clothing?

CD: Absolutely! People have no idea just what they are getting themselves into.

Please describe the "unusual aspects" of sex that you enjoy.

CD: I enjoy being verbally dominated. I find that to be incredibly sexy. Obviously, no one wants to be injured during sex, but I do enjoy the dom/sub dichotomy. As a sub, which is my preference, I enjoy being completely dominated. In my normal life, I have so many responsibilities. I have to be in control, maintain balance and have structure in my life. It's relaxing to have a day where you are not in control of anything. You go with the flow and allow someone else to take the lead. It's very freeing and gratifying in a very psychological, as well as physical way.

Some believe that BDSM is equal parts psychological and physical. Would you agree?

CD: I feel that BDSM is even more psychological than it is physical. If someone is just sitting their, hitting me with a flail, it is going to do absolutely nothing to me. The dom needs to be verbal and assertive with me. That's the way to get me into the scene and into that particular frame of mind.

Once the verbal aspects about BDSM come into play, I wonder what it is that turns on in your brain.

CD: I'm not sure. The first time I ever did any type of play like that was on camera. I thought I'd be open-minded and give it a try. If I didn't like it, I wouldn't ever dabble with it again. It turned out that not only did I like it, but I really liked it. It woke me up.

How did you find your way into that style of sex? Most of us had "regular" sex in the back of cars as teens and young adults. The sex that we all start out with is miles away from BDSM expression.

CD: Exactly! For the most part, even in the beginning of my porn career, sex was more traditional. Boy/girl or girl/girl, is was all very emotionally and physically traditional. BDSM is just an elevated type of sex that some people will evolve into. It's not for everyone, but it is for me.

Since you are an obvious fan of BDSM sex, do you enjoy traditional sex as well?

CD: BDSM is emotionally and physically exhausting, so yes, I do enjoy other forms of sex too. I wouldn't be able to handle nothing but BDSM on a daily basis. It's exhausting. It's awesome and cathartic, but I couldn't go through that everyday. Some days, I just want to have regular sex and have great orgasms with a partner. There's a place in my life for all types of sex.

How can people enjoy alternative styles of sex?

CD: I think more people would like varied sexual experience if they could get themselves to a place where they were open to it. Some people may think it's dirty or that only a certain type of person has alternative styles of sex. There are also emotional and cultural things that keep us from trying new sexual experiences and branching out. Some people may also have concerns about being judged for liking what they like or for revealing secret fantasies or fetishes.

There is even a stigma concerning same-sex sexual experiences as well.

CD: A lot of people have strong religious beliefs about same sex experiences. Many people truly feel that homosexual people are going to hell. Some may feel that being homosexual, whether lesbian or gay, may, in a way, be damning yourself to eternal horribleness. If that was your belief, you would never feel free to try out your same-sex fantasies in reality.

Describe your first lesbian experience.

CD: I was actually quite young. We used to play house together and would bring each other to orgasm. For the first few years of doing this, we would say, "I'm the boyfriend and you're the girlfriend... or husband/wife." That was all we knew of sex. Sex had to be between a man and a woman. Once we got older, we started learning about lesbians through television and pop culture. At that point, we stopped playing with each other sexually.

At what age did you first have sex with a boy?

CD: I was seventeen.

What type of woman turns you on?

CD: I'm drawn to a woman that is very feminine, soft, gentle, and girly. On the flip side, I prefer my men to be rugged and masculine. I don't want a feminine man or a masculine woman. I love the difference. I want my partner to be the epitome of femininity or masculinity.

Porn serves so many valuable purposes. For one, porn helps people spice up their love lives and refrains from the boredom of having monotonous sex. Would you agree?

CD: This is true. Not everyone is super creative and that's fine. It takes all sorts of different people to make the world awesome. People desire variety and watching a porn may help achieve that by showcasing new positions, the use of toys, or role playing.

Did you ever come across pornography in your youth that turned you on?

CD: Yes, I found a Playboy that a friend of mine had under his bed. It was so vanilla when I think about it now. It had two women looking like they were going to kiss. It was the first image I had ever seen depicting the type of thing I liked to do. I was thrilled to find people that were just like me. I was so confused about my sexuality, at that point. I also saw a porn where two girls had a food fight in a kitchen and then had sex. I was thrilled beyond belief to see that too. It was so wonderful for me. I thought to myself, "I'm not a freak. I'm not weird. Other people are doing this too."

As a sex professional, could you offer our readers some advice for spicing up their love life?

CD: There are so many ways of spicing up a sexual relationship, although the main word of advice would be to maintain an open and honest dialogue with your partner. You should have a comfort level in your relationship that allows you to reveal your fantasies and desires without ridicule or judgment. Revealing your inner most desires can be a very vulnerable revelation that must be treated respectfully, whether you are comfortable with their particular desire or not. Doing that, at times, can be harder than it sounds. Open communication is a must.

So, we are guessing that the people who are not comfortable confiding their fantasies to their partners are the ones that patronize your movies, website, and live shows?

CD: Absolutely! It's partially the reason why porn is a multi-billion dollar industry. There are some online fans that will pay outrageous amounts of money just to view the folds of my feet because their partner won't comply. In fact, many of my fans are married and have, what I consider, very vanilla fantasies. My advice is to take baby steps and try things out. Be vocal. Be honest. Communicate with your partner. Everybody has a fantasy and a secret world that they would love to explore with a trusting partner. Go for it!

In fact, some women may not even know what their own vagina looks like.

CD: That is so true! Some people are total strangers to themselves. Get a mirror and have a look. You're beautiful.

Do you feel that porn has a broader spectrum of beauty than the mainstream world?

CD: The industry comes in all different shapes and sizes. That's the absolute beauty of it. There are big boobs, little boobs, saggy boobs, blondes, brunettes, cellulite, big asses, narrow asses, tall chicks, short chicks, fat chicks, young chicks, and old chicks. You name it, the porn world embraces it. It's all encompassing and it's all wonderful. The mainstream media casts a much smaller box of what's considered beautiful that people try to fit into. Porn is much more female positive. Remember, there is no Photoshop on film. We are authentic, fully exposed, and out there.

Do you dress up at home?

CD: I love dressing up at home. I enjoy wearing 40 and 50's style clothing. I love wearing pin-up girl outfits and swing dancing. I am so girly. I'll rock a pencil skirt and a sexy cat eye anytime. Femininity is a lost art in modern times. I love for women to be women and look classic. At some Los Angeles clubs, I feel more feminine and attractive in my ladylike clothing that shows off my waistline than the girls who are dressed so promiscuously. Somehow being as naked as possible in public has become apart of the modern club culture. I'm going to absolutely stand out from the pack for an entirely different set of reasons. And, the whole naked look is not flattering on every body.

Do you feel that the mainstream world borrows from the adult world?

CD: Absolutely! Whatever the porno look is for that particular time will undoubtedly trickle down into pop culture. For example, back in the day, when there were some issues with certain STDs, people started shaving their pubic hair for health reasons. Then, the mainstream world took notice and followed suit. Now, that that isn't so much of an issue anymore, bush is back. It's back in mainstream too. It all trickles down, even to the clothing shops in the mall. The mainstream world even copies porn star makeup applications too- smoky eyes, fake eyelashes, pouty lips.

You just celebrated your birthday! Did you have fun?

CD: Yes! I went to the beach for the first time. Whenever I came to Los Angeles before moving here, I was busy working and never had any free time. I would sleep and work and sleep and work. Now, I'm limiting my work time and am playing tourist, going out with friends, and experiencing what this great city is all about. My birthday was a great time. And my workload is only getting better and better. In fact, I've only just begun!

****

Eva Karera

Birth Date: May 6

Hometown: Belgium

Height: 5'7"

Weight: 125 lbs.

Movies:

MILFS and Titties- New Sensations

Ass Fucking Moms- Rosebud

Ask Mommy 3- Zero Tolerance

Anal Mother Fuckers- Devil's Angel

All Star Anal Sluts 3- Evil Angel

Thanks for taking the time to talk with us. Is today your day off?

EK: Yes and no. It doesn't really work that way for me. Sometimes, at the last minute, I'm called onto set to fill in for a person for various reasons, like illness. Surprise shoots are known to pop up from time to time, so planning a day off becomes quite difficult.

Do you participate in webcam shows?

EK: I used to do them in Europe but don't really do them any more. There are so many web cam girls out there, lots of competition. Also, some webcam girls do their shows for free which is something I do not understand. It is also a lot of work. You must decide what is good and what people are looking for. There is so much more work and time that goes into creating a good show than people realize.

Girls really participate in free webcam shows? That must make it terrible for girls trying to earn a living.

EK: I don't understand it either. Many of the girls that perform in free webcam shows are the girls that need attention to validate themselves. They simply give themselves away and then wonder why no one is making any money. That also makes it difficult for other girls to compete. Who can compete with free? I have many other things to do, so I don't really miss webcamming.

Competition in the webcam market is fierce these days too. Many, if not most of porn's professional performers are supplementing their income with webcam shows.

EK: The market was better a few years ago when there were less people doing it. Before I moved to the United States, like four or five years ago, I would invest one or two hours putting together a sexy show. Everybody is complaining that there is no more money in porn, but I don't agree. There is still money to be earned.

With porn, it seems as though there is an influx of new girls that pop up every day. How do you feel about that?

EK: It's true; every day there seems to be a new girl, although most of them only stay in for a few weeks. Companies also want to show off the new girl until she isn't new anymore. Companies don't want to invest in the big named stars as much as they used to. There are hardly any contract girls left in our industry. Most companies have gotten rid of all of their contract girls, in favor of hiring new girls.

What year did you get started in the adult industry?

EK: I started in summer of 2007. My first scene was in Europe. From 2007 until now, eight years, so much has changed. Back at that time, most of the girls I knew were shooting every day, if not two scenes per day. The girls were very busy. That was before social media. People also knew everyone too. The industry seemed much tighter and closer. There was also no selfies, no Twitter and so on. Access to your fans wasn't the same as it is now.

What was it like performing in Europe?

EK: It was very difficult shooting in Europe. I didn't shoot every day. Since nothing was being shot in Belgium, my homeland, I had to travel abroad. So, for me to shoot one scene, sometimes it would take me three or four days of travel to get to my job. That was at my cost too. I had to take a train, travel with my big suitcase and it was very difficult to manage it all. I did all of that for one scene. I went to Paris, Budapest, Italy, and many other places. For the first eight months, I traveled to many places in Europe.

What was your first professional scene like?

EK: My first scene was shot in Paris. I wasn't afraid or intimidated because I had been performing in live sex shows at swinger's clubs. Having sex in front of people wasn't a big deal to me. What was different was all the lights and people directing you into sexual positions. I had to get used to that.

That must have been extremely exhausting for you.

EK: It was. It was at that point that I said to myself, if I don't move to United States, I'm going to have to find something else to do. From there, I would book trips to Los Angeles for two or three months at a time, working as much as I could. I got more involved in our industry that way and met more people.

Do you prefer the way the industry is now or back in 2007 when you started?

EK: Well, from a personal standpoint, I like it better now. Back in 2007, I was working at another job, had my own store and wasn't doing porn exclusively as my career. Life was very busy for me back then. I was going back and forth.

What type of store did you own?

EK: My shop sold sexy jewelry and lingerie. Many of my clients were swingers. That was my introduction to that lifestyle. I became more comfortable with myself.

How was your transition to America?

EK: It was a challenge. When I decided to move out of my country, it was a big adjustment. My town was very very small. Los Angeles is huge in comparison. I left everything behind and only traveled with my suitcase.

Did you have any friends or anyone to help you assimilate?

EK: No, I did it all by myself.

Wow! That is so courageous. We admire your courage.

EK: Thank you. It's an exciting part of life. I grew up in such a small village. Even as a teenager, I longed for adventure. During winter, it was so cold and we had to stay in. There was lots of snow. We had one bus that would take us to the closest city. That was it. It would travel once per week. Even then, I thought to myself, "I need to get the fuck out of here!" Every time it would snow, I was ready to go. I wanted to go. I needed a town that had energy. My heart and my dreams were too big for my little town.

What year did you move to Los Angeles?

EK: I moved to Los Angeles in 2011. It took me some time to feel at home in Los Angeles. Los Angeles is so specific and is such a big city. You have to drive everywhere. It's not like New York. In New York, you can walk everywhere. In Los Angeles, you must have a car.

Your English is quite good. Did you learn English in Belgium of here?

EK: I took language in school, but learned most of it here. When I first arrived here, I even found it difficult to communicate with my agent. I still have a very strong accent. I started to watch movies and read books in English to learn more.

Where else have you lived?

EK: I've also loved in Turkey and in Egypt where I taught scuba diving. I learned more language there, but it was not American English. Actually, it ruined the English I had already learned. It was all mixed up.

What was it like teaching scuba diving? What a surprise!

EK: I started doing it for fun and then got certified to instruct. I've dived more than one thousand times. I love it. It was such a switch from being in the ocean, in cold water, lots of gear to being glamorous on a porn set. I am full of surprises.

Do you scuba dive here?

EK: I've dived in many parts of Mexico, the Bahamas, Miami and lots of other places but haven't dived in a while. I plan to do it soon. I won't teach ever again, but I will practice scuba for fun. I love being at the beach. The water is soothing. I just need to move. My body must move. I must explore, learn and be active.

It seems as if your entire world doesn't revolve around the porn industry. Is that true?

EK: Yes. I believe it is important for a person to have multiple interests. I love sports and outdoor activities. There has to be a good balance in life to remain happy. I also love going to the gym. Balance is the key.

Do you prefer working with established talent or with new talent?

EK: I prefer working with people that are professionals and that have been around for a while. Scenes become more complicated if the other person doesn't know what they are doing, especially with girls. I don't want to be a teacher. I want to be a great performer. It is fun working with new people, already established performers. That is exciting.

Who are some of your favorite performers to work with?

EK: Lexington Steele, Manuel Ferrara, Erik Everhard, Ramon Nomar. Those are real men that know how to fuck me right.

How did you decide upon your stage name, Eva Karera?

EK: I wanted a name that was easy to spell and remember. I chose to spell Karera the way I did just in case I wanted to trademark the name later on. I didn't want it to be too similar to the car.

We loved your work in *Avengers XXX 2: An Axel Braun Parody*- Vivid. Did you have a pleasant experience on set?

EK: Yes, I loved that movie. My character was named Red Guardian. I really loved my sexy red costume too. My costume was custom made for me. It was the first time I was in a costume and in character in a porn movie. My costume had a zipper on the crotch. My boobs stayed covered. I was told that comic book fans like when the costumes stay on during sex. I thought I was going to be shooting all day and night, but I wasn't. I left the set at 7PM. It was awesome. I got to attend my Christmas party afterwards.

Whom did you work with?

EK: I performed with Seth Gamble. We've worked together before. We had a great time that day. I really had a fun time shooting that movie.

Do you prefer spit or lube?

EK: Spit! I prefer spit. I don't like feeling all greasy and oily from the lube. Men usually prefer spit too.

We've seen you in a fair amount of Gonzo and interracial movies, but hardly any features. It was nice seeing you that way. You have a talent for acting.

EK: I would love to work in more features. The problem is my accent. My accent is quite strong and some people are not interested in shooting that. American movies, features especially, prefer American performers. I think that porn should branch out to include more foreign actresses in feature roles.

What was it like working with director Axel Braun?

EK: It was great. He's very talented and definitely knows what he is doing. He knows how to create a great porn movie that people want to enjoy. He wins many awards for good reason. I'd love the opportunity to work with him again.

What is your favorite type of sex?

EK: I love shooting anal and DP sex scenes. I'm also cast in many interracial movies too. Actually, my first scene was anal. I prefer really energetic sex. One guy may get tired after a while, but with two guys or more, the energy is spread out.

Besides having amazing sex, what is another fun aspect about the adult industry?

EK: I enjoy being glamorous and beautiful on camera. I enjoy being someone's fantasy girl. The idea of people masturbating to me gets me excited.

What aspects don't you enjoy?

EK: I don't enjoy the term MILF. I am not a mother. I've never been a mother. I have no plans for motherhood. I don't like this term at all. I am a sexy woman. That is what I am. I also don't like the idea of incest porn either (taboo/family relations). I think that is gross, wrong and is socially irresponsible. That is not ok. We should not act as if it is ok. In porn, people are obviously not related. Hopefully, people don't blur the lines in the real world and act on it because it's what they see the industry doing. I don't want to participate in those types of scenes.

Where do you prefer your cumloads?

EK: Although I don't like messing up my beautiful makeup, I do enjoy facials. I also like spitting cum onto my boobs. That's always a sexy look. Don't you think?

****

Kendra Lust

Birth Date: September 18

Hometown: Detroit, Michigan

Height: 5'3" 1/2

Weight: 121 lbs.

Measurements: 34D-25-36

Movies:

Kendra Lust 1- Naughty America

Kendra Lust Fucks Couples- ArchAngel Productions

Kendra Lust vs. Lisa Ann- Third Degree Films

All MILF- Fornic8 Films

Kendra Lust's Big Ass Army- Zero Tolerance

What made you choose adult entertainment as a career choice?

KL: Porn is something that I've always wanted to do. In my twenties, I took a more traditional route and went to school, earning a nursing degree. In my thirties, I thought, 'I'm ready for this. I'm ready to unleash my wild side and roll with it!'

Did you have an established career as a nurse before making the leap into porn?

KL: Yes, I did. I'm still a register nurse although I'm not currently practicing.

What turns you off?

KL: Men who turn me off are ones that are too cocky. Really, bad attitudes don't serve anybody well. Bad hygiene is also a no-no. Having stinky armpits and bad breath is just horrible in general. I also don't like men who don't manscape their area. Too much hair down there is just not appealing. No mushrooms in the grass please.

What is your preferred time of day to have sex?

KL: I'm the type of woman who loves morning sex. I love being woken up by a hard dick penetrating my pussy. The spoon position is great, just slip it in and go for it. Head in the pillow sex is wonderful for hot morning sex. It eliminates the morning breath. (laughing)

If you could fuck anybody on the planet, living or dead, who would it be and why?

KL: That's a good question. There are so many to choose from. Channing Tatum is a really hot actor these days. I'd like to play dirty with him. And since I love bad boys so much, I'd have to go with a gritty pro wrestler. The Rock is pretty hot. Yeah, I'd fuck him!

Is The Rock a good example of the type of bad boy that turns you on?

KL: Well, my ideal guy doesn't necessarily have to be so muscular, although I do like my men to have a little meat on their bones. He definitely has to have broad shoulders, be clean-cut and have tattoos. I love tattoos. A man with a little bit of a wild side turns me on. I really like that. Since I'm rather small, it's good being manhandled every now and again.

Sexually, do you prefer men or women?

KL: If I had a choice, I prefer men. However, my favorite thing is starting with a female and ending with a male. I find both to be delicious.

Which male performer fucks you the best and why?

KL: I've been such a lucky girl that I can't pinpoint just one guy. Really, they've all been great. Keiran Lee was really good. Manuel Ferrara is also incredible, as was Johnny Castle and Mark Davis. There is a particular type of guy that I look for in my personal life, but in the bedroom, I love and need the variety.

Which female performer has the yummiest tasting pussy?

KL: So far, I'd have to say that Kendall Karson has a scrumptious tasting pussy. When I worked with her, she tasted so good that I couldn't stop smacking my lips. I definitely enjoyed her. Jayden Jaymes also has a yummy tasting pussy. Both of those girls are hot!

So, does that mean you are more turned on by brunettes?

KL: I don't have a particular type of woman that I'm attracted to. What I do like is a woman with curves and confidence. Blondes, brunettes, it really doesn't matter. All are good with me.

In your professional life, do you enjoy working with the younger talent, or do you prefer fucking the seasoned players?

KL: Honestly, it all depends on my mood. At times, I like the guys that know exactly what they are doing. They can toss me around the room and really fuck me hard in great positions. Other times, I like the young guys because I get to be in the driver's seat and do some damage.

Are you a practicing cougar on and off camera?

KL: I would say that I'm always practicing, whether it's on camera or off camera. My sexual appetite is incredibly strong so I'm always on the look out. The guy that I'm seeing right now is around my age. He's working out well. But, every now and then, I'm known for sticking my kitty claws into fresh meat.

What is your method of seduction?

KL: I don't really play hard to get. Instead, if I want something, I take it. I'm very confident, so that helps me get whomever I want. My foreplay and oral skills are also quite good. That does the trick. And, I love flirting with my eyes. That's always fun and sexy. Eyes are the most seductive part of a woman. I especially love maintaining eye contact when giving head.

What are some of your guilty pleasures?

KL: I love watching *Jersey Shore*. It's such a train wreck that I can't peel my eyes away from it. I also enjoy working out and going to strip clubs with my friends. All of those things turn me on.

Are you known for bringing your work home with you?

KL: Yes, there have been a few occasions where I brought my work home with me. Absolutely! I love sharing my new friends with my boyfriend. It's fun bringing a third in if the chemistry is right. Currently, we're taking applications! (laughing)

Do you have rules or guidelines that you abide by when engaging in three-way sex with your lover?

KL: Sure, we talk about our boundaries. Since we haven't really done anal sex ourselves, that is a no-no. I wouldn't be okay with that. Everything else is oaky, although anal sex is going to be something that we share with each other.

Are you sexually wilder on or off screen?

KL: I'm about the same. I really love sex on and off camera and really do my best to put out a good scene. I may not open up to the camera as much as I should because I'm really into it. All I can say is that the sex my fans see is genuine. Opening up to the camera is something I'm going to have to work on. My sexual appetite is strong either way. Onscreen, I'm *really* enjoying myself.

Are you into bondage at all?

KL: Light bondage is fun. Butt smacking, a little bit of choking and nipple clamps can be a good time. Being tied up can also be fun. And spit, I love spit. Spitting really turns me on. But, as far as a lot of pain goes, I'm not really okay with that. I like to feel like I'm on a tight wire. I can teeter over the edge, but then I'm pulled back. I like to switch out between being dominate and submissive.

What do you think it is about the MILF/Cougar genre that drives men wild?

KL: Men like a woman who is confident and skilled in her sexuality. In my twenties, I really wasn't. I though I was, but I wasn't. Now, I know exactly what I want and know how to get it. And, I'm not afraid to take it. I think men also enjoy a woman who actually looks like a women. Mature women are more aware of their bodies and have more sexual experience and skills to work with.

What are some of your pet peeves?

KL: Overconfident people annoy me. People who are not polite also irritate me. For instance, if there is heavy traffic and I let somebody in, I expect a friendly wave. If I don't get that, it really ticks me off. Sometimes people forget how to use their manners. I practice the golden rule. Some people need to brush up on their social etiquette skills. Materialistic people are also quite disturbing to me. Really, do you need $1,000 shoes?

What is your sexiest physical attribute?

KL: My legs and butt are quite sexy. My legs are thick and muscular and my butt is solid. I work out three days per week, incorporating weightlifting and cardio.

Do you care that you are categorized as a MILF/Cougar performer?

KL: It doesn't really bother me. In porn, you are bound to fall into one category or another. Either you are really young, or you are a cougar/MILF. Titles don't define who I am. I'm sexy either way.

Please describe Kendra Lust, porn star.

KL: I'm very sexual, confident and am a sporty porn star. I'm the type of girl that you can take out to a ball game or dress up for a romantic evening out. I'm just a regular chick who loves hardcore sex. Some people have called me a sexy tomboy.

What makes you unique as a performer? What special qualities do you bring to the table?

KL: I'm a very filthy talker and enjoy talking dirty during sex. I'm also very appreciative of my fans and take time to respond to them. My fans are awesome. I really appreciate them.

It sounds like you are a very approachable porn star. What is the best way for fans to approach you? .

KL: Just come up and say hi. As long as you are respectful and cool with me, I'll be cool with you. I'm very approachable. I'd never be the type to snub my fans.

What makes seasoned cougars sexier than the younger starlets?

KL: Nothing against the youngsters, but we, seasoned players, know what we want and we know how to fuck! Come on now, how could a young girl compete with that?

****

Leya Falcon

Birth Date: March 3

Hometown: Las Vegas, Nevada

Height: 5'6"

Weight: 126 lbs.

Measurements: 34DD-25-38

Movies:

Anal Sluts Like it Raw- Allure Films

Big Titty Mamas- Black Market

Big Tits- Desire Films

Big Tit Fanatic 3- Elegant Angel

Ass Factor 4- Ass Factory

What made you decide to enhance your breasts? They are spectacular, by the way!

LF: Since I was born in Vegas, it seems as though everywhere I'd look there'd be big, fake tits. And, while growing up, I even remember Barbie having great, big tits. So I wanted to have big, fake tits too. They never popped up naturally, so I went out and bought them.

Did you lose sensitivity in your boobs when you got them enhanced?

LF: My boobs have never really been all that sensitive to begin with. They are pretty much decoration for me unless it's a turn on for someone else to play with them. My boobs look pretty and make me feel very sexy.

You are adorned with many interesting tattoos. Do any of them have specific or significant meaning?

LF: Pretty much all of my tattoos have significant meaning for me. I have my daughter's name on one shoulder, and a picture of Jack Skellington from the *Nightmare Before Christmas* on the other. I have a skull on my back, which is a logo for my favorite music group ever, *Bone Thugs in Harmony*. My kitty's name is on my back. I had her since I was a child and she just passed in 2010 of old age. I have a pair of handcuffs on my right leg because I collect handcuffs and love rough sex. That tattoo reminds me of being Slave Leya because I love Star Wars, hot bitches and kinky sex. I have a bleeding black heart on the back of my neck and a tattoo on my arms that reads, Love is Pain. I was eighteen when I got that one, right after I smoked a fat joint. That tattoo was probably not the best idea. I regret that one.

Are there any other tattoos that you regret?

LF: Yes, I also regret the tattoo around my finger with my husband's name on it. Right now, I'm in the process of getting that one removed.

Which performers have been able to push you beyond your sexual limits?

LF: I've been pushed beyond my sexual limit by a sexual situation, not by an individual person. I once did a scene for Kink.com, for a project called *Public Disgrace*. I really loved it, except for the first part of the scene. In that scenario, a bunch of people watched me getting fucked while being able to touch me at the same time. I'm very ADD (attention deficit disorder), so having more than a few sets of hands on me at once completely confuses me and throws me off. I can't focus on actually enjoying myself. That definitely pushed my limits in a good way. Honestly, I don't have very many sexual limits. When having sex, I just like to concentrate on enjoying myself instead of having too many things going on at once. It's too much sensory overload for me to handle.

After all was said and done, how did the scene turn out?

LF: It turned out to be one of my favorite scenes ever shot. I had to call out 'stop' a couple of times, but once they chilled out a little bit, the scene turned out to be one of my hottest to date. It was rough, kinky and dirty. They even mopped the floor with my hair. It was crazy.

Which male performer has the most skillful cock?

LF: Tommy Pistol has a very skillful cock, despite the fact that it isn't too big. He does very well with what he has. I enjoy performing with him to the fullest.

In that particular instance, bigger doesn't necessarily mean better.

LF: I want men to be mean, rough and dirty with their cocks. Some men with big cocks are lazy lovers and may not know what to do with it. What a waste. I want men to rough me up, smack my ass and pull my hair. Some guys are like, 'Yeah, I have a big cock. Just shut up and fuck it!'

Which female performer has the most skillful tongue?

LF: I haven't had the chance to perform with many females, which I'm very sad about because I love females. Since I fuck cocks on set, they don't pair me up with girls very often. However, Sheena Shaw is a lot of fun. She has a great ass and an amazing tongue.

So, is it safe to assume that you enjoy females in your personal life?

LF: Yes! I always tell people I'm 97.3% lesbian and the other 2.7% is reserved for penis. As far as bodies are concerned, I prefer women. I love playing with them and touching them. I do love me some cock though.

Since you love 97.3% of women and only 2.7% of that equation is reserved for dick, do you enjoy

chicks with dicks (transsexuals)? To us, it would seem the ideal/logical choice.

LF: No, I have nothing against transsexuals. They just don't happen to turn me on. If I want to be with a girl, I want to be with one who is 100%. I want her to have the tits, ass, a pretty face and a tasty pussy. I need to connect with her feminine qualities. If I want a guy, he has to be 100% man. He needs to manhandle me and all that shit.

What would be your ideal type of women?

LF: Just take a look at Lisa Ann. She is all the woman I could ever need or want. She has huge tits, a beautiful face, a thick ass, and is good at fucking.

So, do you prefer brunettes over blondes?

LF: Yes, because I'm a blonde and opposites attract. I do like blondes too but prefer a person that doesn't look too much like me.

Have you ever had the opportunity to work with Lisa Ann?

LF: No, I haven't. I'm dying for the opportunity though. She's going on my wish list. I can't wait to be her little fuck doll. I don't want to tear my teeth into her. I want her to tear her teeth into me. Lisa Ann, if you're reading this, you're on my To-Do List. I'll let that hot bitch do anything to me.

Do blondes really have more fun?

LF: Hell yeah they do! I always have myself a good ol' fucking time!

Speaking of fun, where's the wildest place you've ever had sex?

LF: I once had sex behind a church. Yeah, I know. I'm a whore. I went to a Christian school when I was younger that had a church attached to it. So, I ditched school one day and went behind the church to fuck. I fucked that boy good too.

What is your favorite way to reach orgasm?

LF: I need heavy-duty penetration with something extremely hard. As long as the toy or the cock is hard and pounding the fuck out of me, it will work.

Have you ever experienced a squirting orgasm while being pounded?

LF: Squirting is what I'm known for. About 98% of the time, I'm going to squirt. When I'm filming, it's easy for me to have squirting orgasms. There have only been a few times when I was unable to squirt on screen because the scene was being shot so strangely. I couldn't get off and it pissed me off!

Can you make yourself squirt while masturbating?

LF: Yes, I can! So long as I have a toy, my pussy is going to gush!

It's a wonder you haven't shriveled up and died from pussy dehydration.

LF: I'm always hydrated. I love water and Diet Coke. I have a really wet mouth and get really sweaty during sex. No matter the situation, it seems as though there is always fluid dripping off me.

Are you publicly noticed by your fans?

LF: It has happened a couple of times. At the AVN Awards, everyone seemed to know who I was. I was shocked since I've only been in the industry for about a year. I had all these people grabbing at me, taking pictures with me and telling me how much they love me. It was crazy. They said things like, "I really like your work." But, it has been awkward when fans approach me when I'm with my daughter. Time and place people.

What is the most thoughtful item given to you by a fan?

LF: Recently, I got a new iPod, thank god! My old one broke. Since I drive back and forth to Los Angeles for work, I need to have my music. I also got a cat necklace that is made of black diamonds, since my previous cat and my current cat, Ms. Yoda, are black. That gift was really fucking special.

When you are not working, what are you doing?

LF: I work a lot, even if I'm not shooting. I strip for fun and have been doing that since I was eighteen. I also write a sexy blog. From sun up to sun down, I'm active.

Who is on your fantasy fuck list?

LF: Lisa Ann. She's all I need.

Would you like to branch out and perform in more feature driven productions or do you prefer working in Gonzos?

LF: I want to do it all. As long as I get fucked in the end, I'm happy. I've only shot one parody so far, but had a great time doing it. I played a stripper in *This Ain't Terminator XXX* for LFP Video. I'd love to shot more parodies. They are so hilarious.

Why did you get into the adult business?

LF: I love attention. I need attention and I love to fuck. I wanted all the attention. I guess I got my wish.

****

Natalia Starr

Birth Date: March 22

Hometown: Poland

Height: 5'8"

Weight: 125 lbs.

Measurements: 34D-26-34

Movies:

Sexual Desires of Natalia Starr- New Sensations

Mommy & Me 9- Filly Films

Housewife 1 on 1 #34- Naughty America

Dirty Blondes 2- Elegant Angel

Only Natalia Starr- Cherry Pimps

What attracted you to the adult industry?

NS: My sister, Natasha Starr, was already in the industry for about one year before I decided to join. I found the industry to be fascinating and loved all the attention she was getting. I wanted some of that for myself. I couldn't wait to be apart of that too.

So far, are you glad that you made the leap into porn?

NS: Yes, I love it! It's been a wonderful experience.

Whom have you had the pleasure of working with?

NS: I've been spoiled. I've had the opportunity to work with so many different people. Luckily, I haven't had any bad porn experiences. Actually, my first lesbian sex scene was in porn.

Wow! Who was the lucky lady?

NS: I worked with the beautiful, Brett Rossi. She showed me the exact way to please a woman, since I really didn't have any prior experience. She was my first. The scene surprised me. She really turned me on. Before then, I didn't realize that I could have sexual feelings for a woman.

Prior to porn, you had zero experience with women?

NS: Well, not zero. I made out with a few girls and touched a few pairs of breasts but nothing further than second base. I had never gone all the way with a girl before Brett.

According to Brett Rossi, how was your pussy eating skills?

NS: She liked it! That girl was definitely not complaining!

What about you? Did it make you feel strange to have a woman going down on you?

NS: No, not really. It felt the same. There really wasn't a clear difference between a man or a woman going down on me. What I can say is that I really liked it.

After having been with women, what would you say is your favorite position?

NS: Sixty-nine! I simply love the taste, feel and look of two women eating vagina at the same time. That is so hot!

With whom did you perform your first boy/girl sex scene?

NS: My first boy/girl sex scene was with Marco Banderas. He was great. I got to play the part of a cheerleader. I was so hyper, excited, and really got into character. Actually, nobody on set knew it was my first scene. Everybody was shocked and said I was a natural. I just said, 'Hey, I *have* had sex before.' (laughing)

What are some major differences between porn sex and personal sex?

NS: There aren't any big differences. You just have to open up a bit more so that the camera can see all the good stuff. You also have to learn how to find the light and know your attractive angles.

How many people had you fucked prior to your first scene?

NS: I was always in a relationship, so there wasn't much opportunity for me to get with too many guys. There were a few encounters, but not too many. I plan on changing that.

After having your first taste of pussy, and several bites thereafter, would you consider yourself bi-sexual?

NS: No, I would consider myself bi-curious. Although I love women, I couldn't see myself in a relationship with one. Don't get me wrong, I love fondling a woman's body. I go crazy for women's asses, titties and the taste of pussy. Women taste so fucking good.

How did your friends react to your career choice?

NS: They weren't surprised. They knew it was only a matter of time before I dove into porn. I've always been very open and honest with my friends. Thankfully, they are the type of people that will stand behind me and support my choices.

What about your ex-boyfriends, how did they react?

NS: A week before I bought my ticket to leave New York and come to Los Angeles to meet with my agent, I talked with my boyfriend, ex-boyfriend now, about my decision. Again, I was honest with him from the start. I knew he wasn't going to be alright with it, so I broke things off with him. I said, 'This is my decision. This is what I'm going to do.' I pretty much said sayonara!

What are the advantages of being a teenage porn star?

NS: Right now, the porn industry likes the young girl look and girls with natural breasts. Luckily, I have both. Audiences seem to like either the young girl look or the MILFS. The space in between is a bit gray. Since I am so new, so cute and so young, it seems like the porn world can't get enough of me. Actually, I can't get enough of them either.

Have you found that there are also disadvantages of being a teenage porn star?

NS: Some people feel that they can take advantage of young girls since they lack experience. They may ask you to add on other tasks for your scenes, even though you weren't technically booked for it. They also try to play around with our rates, and see what else they can get for free. This is why I love the agency I am affiliated with. If there is ever a question or I feel weird or uncertain about a situation, I can call them up and they with explain everything to me or fix the problem. My agency has my back. I may be young, but I am not naive like some of the other performers that are my same age.

Before porn, please describe the wildest sexual experience you ever had.

NS: I once had three-way sex with my best and her boyfriend. I only kissed and fondled her, nothing too crazy. However, we did end up sharing him. It was a great time. It all started because I heard them having sex in the corner of the room and it turned me on. I asked if I could join them and they said yes. They made me so horny. That was a hot experience.

Are there performers that you greatly admired?

NS: I admire Jenna Jameson. She's turned a sex career into something much greater. She's also an outstanding business woman and has really boosted herself up. Now, she's a household name. Even if you aren't a porn fan, you know the name, Jenna Jameson. You have to admire a woman like that.

Of the performers who are still active, which ones would you enjoy working with?

NS: I'd love to work with Asa Akira, Alexis Texas and Allie Haze. I'm in love with Allie. She's such a stand out performer. Actually, I haven't really been booked with the top porn talent yet. Instead, my agency has been booking me with girls that are on my same level. I guess I have to work my way up.

What about male performers? Who are you dying to work with?

NS: I would absolutely love the opportunity to work with Manuel Ferrara. He is so sexy. And, the man has a great looking penis. I've never worked with him and have never met him. I just know his face, his body and his reputation. He's so hot! He's on the top of my list! I want his dick so badly right now.

What are some of your guilty pleasures?

NS: I love watching the sitcom, *The Big Bang Theory*. I could watch that show any time, any place. Watching that show is one of my favorite things to do. Really, the show is hilarious!

Do you have any secret porn crushes?

NS: James Deen. You can put him on my list too. He's a sexy white boy. James Deen is my next victim. The way I see it, it's only a matter of time.

What separates you from other starlets?

NS: My personality is unique. I'm very quirky and have a funny personality. I am happy and full of life. I think that my playfulness puts people at ease. My quirkiness would definitely be one quality that would separate me from the pack.

Please describe your ideal type of woman?

NS: I love rare Spanish girls that have colored eyes, big butts, fat titties, small bodies and dark skin. Emy Reyes is a Spanish girl in the industry that turns me on. She doesn't have the colored eyes, but she has everything else. Selena Rose would be another solid example of the type of girl I like. Funny, the look that turns me on is the exact opposite of what I am. I'm a tall blonde who loved short brunettes.

And what about men? What type of men make you wet?

NS: Any man that looks like Manuel Ferrara will turn me on. I love dark features. In fact, I'm not really into blondes with blue eyes. Also, I love a man with a little meat on their bones and a big dick!

What is a surprise fact about you that might not be common knowledge?

NS: I'm kind of crude and gassy like a boy. I burp and fart all the time. I'm not very polished.

What is your favorite type of sex?

NS: Any sex that makes me cum is good sex. I like to start things off slow and passionately and have it lead to really aggressive sex. I love hugging kissing and smashing our bodies together.

When is your preferred time to have sex-- morning, noon or night?

NS: I enjoy fucking in the afternoon. Daytime fucking is hot! Afterwards, I can roll over and take a nap.

How does it make you feel to know that people around the world are having sex to your movies and with your image?

NS: It makes me feel so hot and powerful. Really, the thought turns me on more than you can even imagine. I possess the power to excite people and make them cum. Really, what is better than that?

Do you have any parting words for your fans?

NS: Stay tuned. I'm not going anywhere!

****

Nikita Von James

Birth Date: April 11

Hometown: Siberia, Russia

Height: 5'5"

Weight: 110 lbs.

Measurements: 34DD-25-36

Movies:

Deep Pussy 2: MILFS- Evil Angel

Cougar Club 4- Third Degree Films

Big Tits- Desire Films

Busty Office MILFS 4- Third Degree Films

Big Tit MILFS 3- Third Degree Films

You have extremely beautiful features. What is your ethnicity?

NVJ: Thank you! I'm 100% Russian and am very proud of my culture.

How does a girl from Siberia land in the adult industry?

NVJ: I've always been curious about the adult industry, even at an early age. In Russia, I stole a video tape from my cousin. I was so turned on by what I saw, but was even more curious about what might be going on behind the scenes. Soon, I finished school in Russia and my mother sent me away to learn English at Cal State Northridge University. I was an exchange student. The year was 1998. I was twenty-one-years old.

Was it a huge culture shock when you first arrived in the San Fernando Valley?

NVJ: When I got here, I felt such a freedom. I felt like I belonged. Later on, I started dancing in strip clubs while continuing to go to school. After that, I joined the adult industry. It all began with baby steps. Now, here I am.

Are there many career opportunities for women in Siberia?

NVJ: Yes, there are but you must have a masters or other professional degree in order to gain employment. It is mandatory. It's funny, while I was in Russia, I didn't really see anything from the adult industry. Now, I know it's there. I know they shoot there and have strip clubs there too.

Have you always been a sexual woman?

NVJ: Yes, from as far back as I can remember. When I was young, I would read sexy books and they would excite me. I've always been curious about my body and my pussy. I knew it was special and could do a lot.

Does your sexuality include pleasuring women?

NVJ: Yes, I love women and am an active bi-sexual. Being in the strip club world for several years, I've definitely been around plenty of sexy women. Imagine all the strippers in the dressing room, changing and getting naked. Of course, we fool around. It is so normal. We enjoy playing with each other backstage, but would also work in tandem together onstage too. Many of the shows I am involved in include more than just one woman.

Please tell us about your first lesbian experience off camera.

NVJ: In Russia, when I was a teen, I wondered what it felt like to kiss a girl. To help me out, my best friend and I began kissing. We didn't know what in the hell we were doing but knew that it felt sexy and naughty. There was a lot of wetness. Another experience happened when I was twenty-one, when I first came to America. A few months in, I was invited to a party where there was a porn star. I can't remember her name now. I was so attracted to her. She was so gorgeous, a little girl with a perfect body. After a few cocktails, we got together.

Got together? Did that include hardcore sex?

NVJ: Yes, we did everything. We licked each other's pussies and really fooled around. I was so shy. I really didn't know what I was doing and was freaking out a little bit. She handled me perfectly, but I felt a little more self-conscious about my skills. I thought to myself, 'Damn, am I doing this right?' Finally, I just let those negative thoughts go and just went with it. That's when it got good!

Was she able to bring you to orgasm?

NVJ: Yes, she did! But guess what, I was able to bring her to orgasm too!

Is it true, do blondes have more fun?

NVJ: Yes, that is true. When I first got to America, I had much darker hair. Monetarily speaking, in the strip clubs, I make much more money as a blonde. When I changed my hair darker again, my income went down a little bit. Blondes are sexy. For some men, it really doesn't matter how the girl looks. If she's blonde, she's cool and she's sexier. I enjoy being blonde but can't play the ditsy role. I'm very educated but definitely understand men's fascination with blondes. Society puts a big emphasis on women with golden hair. When you think about it, not everybody is blonde. There are far more brunettes than blondes. Blondes seem to fit the male fantasy better.

Do blondes with DD tits have even more fun?

NVJ: Oh baby, you have no idea!

What do men love to do with your beautiful boobs?

NVJ: Men love putting their face between my big boobs. On camera, a big favorite is titty fucking. It's fun moving them around their face and their cock, making them slippery with saliva. When I'm with a girl, I prefer her to have big boobs too. There is so much more I can do with them. With smaller boobs, I'm limited.

Since your breast enhancement, do you still have plenty of sensitivity?

NVJ: Yes, but they are less sensitive. My nipples still have a fair amount of sensitivity, so I'm good. I can still receive quite a lot of pleasure.

What type of clothing make you feel sexy?

NVJ: The clothing has to be tight and short. I love wearing mini dresses and mini skirts, with high heels. My entire closet is full of sexy dresses. I also love putting my long legs in tight jeans. Both are sexy looks.

Do you dress up for your lovers?

NVJ: I love dressing up for my lovers. It's so much fun to keep things energetic and spicy.

Do you role-play with your lovers? If so, what type of characters do you like to become?

NVJ: That is one of my favorite things to do. I have so many different outfits. Actually, last night I was surfing the net for more costumes to wear. Right now, I love wearing my cop outfit, my schoolgirl outfit, fetish outfits and bondage outfits. I love being bad when I play. I adore latex clothing and look really good in my Catwoman suit. I also spice it up by wearing sexy boots.

Bondage? Fetish? Latex? Oh my! Does this mean you are more of a dominant lover?

NVJ: On camera, I love being dominant. In my own bedroom, I can be both. It all depends on my mood. In general, I am probably more submissive in the bedroom. Actually, I think I'm more submissive with men and more dominate with women. Many of the women I am sexual with really want me to take the lead. I'm happy to do so.

What is your wildest sexual fantasy?

NVJ: I enjoy the thought of having sex in public. Right now, I'm imagining having sex in Hawaii, near a waterfall. The element of danger or the fear of being caught is a great turn on.

What does the tattoo on your left arm symbolize?

NVJ: All the butterflies on my arm represent all the women in my family. I also have some flowers on my lower back. While dancing, I noticed that every dancer had a tramp stamp on her back. I wanted one too. I wanted to fit in. I don't think of that one as much since I don't ever see it. (laughing)

Is dancing how you manage to stay in such great shape?

NVJ: Yes! I dance for five hours straight, sometimes. On stage, I'm constantly working out my core muscles and am walking around in high heels. My legs have become so toned. It's a great way to stay nice and tight. I still dance to this day.

Please give us the Nikita Von James way of sucking cock.

NVJ: Make it the sloppiest and messiest blowjob that you possibly can. Dry blowjobs are terrible. You must use your hands and your tongue. Stroke his cock, change your tempo from fast to slow, use both hands and give good eye contact. I also enjoy stuffing cocks between my tits and using my tongue while titty fucking. I think you get the picture. (laughing)

Which performer is able to pull the dirty girl out of you?

NVJ: Angelina Valentine turns me into the dirtiest slut imaginable! I'm getting goose bumps just thinking about her. I love working with her. Although I'm usually the classy one, when we work together, something inside of her changes me. We have crazy passion. We are so similar looking, as far as our bodies are concerned. We're polar opposites. I'm the hot blonde while she's the hot brunette.

Who would you love to work with but haven't yet?

NVJ: I'd love the opportunity to work with Evan Stone. He is hilarious and is so much fun. When he's on set, he's such a joy to be around. He makes time on set fly by and is always in a cheerful mood. He's a happy person, loves our industry and has an unbeatable personality. And, the guy can fuck!

Are you a size queen? Does the size of a man's cock really matter that much to you?

NVJ: Yes, it does! I love big cocks. I want to feel stuffed up.

Currently, do you perform in interracial sex scenes?

NVJ: I plan on performing in interracial sex scenes soon, both on set and for my exclusive website. I love black men in my private life too, so this should be fun. There are so many hot black men in our industry to choose from. I can't wait. I think the contrast in our skin colors will be a real turn on for many people. I know I'm looking forward to it!

****

Nina Elle

Birth Date: April 27

Hometown: Germany

Height: 5'5"

Weight: 115 lbs.

Measurements: 34DD-24-36

Movies:

Bang my Step Mom 11- Porn.com

All Prince Yahshua- Zero Tolerance

All About MILFS- Brazzers

Nina Elle id the ArchAngel- Arch Angel Productions

All MILF 2- Fornic8 Films

Is today your day off?

NE: Well, not exactly. After our interview, I'm going to go off and shoot some dominatrix stuff.

Dominatrix stuff? Well good morning to you too! This is a great place for us to begin.

NE: I enjoy participating in dominatrix style stuff. I do it every now and again to reach out to fans, fulfill some more intensive type fantasies and make extra money. Funny enough, I find it to be relaxing in a strange way.

How did you get started with that?

NE: Well, it all started with ball busting. Yes, it is exactly as it sounds. I wasn't sure if I was the type of person that could do something like that to another human being but found out that I was actually really good at it. My struggle came with the thought that I might be hurting these people. I never want to intentionally hurt anyone. Once I figured how much these men loved it, and in some cases needed this form of release, I really got into it. I'm a very good dominatrix now.

"Needed" it? Explain that part.

NE: Yes, most of the men who come to me with ball busting requests are very powerful businessmen. On a daily basis, they have to be 100% in control of their business, their employees, their lives, everything. The pressure they feel is immense. When they are with me, they relinquish all of their control. They have no choice but to submit. For them, my dominatrix play over them strikes the correct balance. For some, it's almost a psychological necessity to maintain a balance between dominance and submission.

What other type of dominatrix work do you participate in?

NE: Humiliation play is popular, dick shaming and caning too. All good stuff. (laughing)

What did you do before porn?

NE: I was a dental hygienist and was a regular 9-5'er. It was a fine job but got boring after a while. I wanted to start earning some extra money too.

Is that when web-camming came into play?

NE: Yes, I started camming in 2010. I started out doing webcam shows and managed to gain a substantially large following. Eventually, they started asking if I performed in porn movies because they wanted to watch my scenes. It was great fun for everyone involved.

You used the word "was", are you still an active cam model?

NE: Now, I'm so busy with other things that I don't do web-camming as much. I'm shooting all the time. It is fun though when I participate with it.

Wait; were you camming and practicing as a dental hygienist at the same time?

NE: The overlap went on for about six months. After that amount of time had passed, I realized how much more I enjoyed camming. The money was better, my schedule was freer, the people were more interesting and I was getting paid to fuck myself. Also, I didn't have creepy guys staring down my smock.

When you were web-camming, did you find that it was a nice way to connect with your fans or was it too personal?

NE: No, I never thought it was too personal. I enjoyed creating things for my fans, fulfilling their fantasies. My web-camming fans formed the foundation for the fan base that I have today. I thought it was a great way to connect and get more personal with my fans. I do wish that I had more time to get back on cams.

Did you ever get bizarre requests from your webcam clients?

NE: Yes, I've definitely had some crazy requests. I once had a person request to watch me pee. That was odd. There was another man that asked to me draw red dots all over my body with a red lipstick. I thought that maybe he had a measles or chickenpox fetish, but no! It was worse, way worse! He then wanted me to shake violently and pretend that my body was being riddled with bullet holes. What?

What was your reaction?

NE: Well, I had to try my best to fulfill his fantasy, so I started thrashing myself around the room and asked him "like this?" And, he said, "No more vigorously!" that was so hilarious. At some point, I started recording that session because I thought it was so crazy and funny. To each their own, I suppose. Well, at least they are living out their fantasy in a responsible way.

So, it seems like you're open to requests and accept them without judgment.

NE: If I can do it, it is within my means and we're not hurting anyone, then why not? Yes, it may be weird for me to imagine painting red dots over my body and pretend that I'm being shot, but whatever, if it makes him happy... why not?

We're guessing that one of the reasons why camming fantasies are so popular is that people may be ashamed or embarrassed to share these kinks with their significant others.

NE: Exactly! Or maybe they enjoy staying anonymous. Now, if they were to ask their wives or girlfriends for that type of play they may be ridiculed, shamed, made fun of or judged. They may never hear the end of it and it may be thrown back at their face during fights. That would be horrible. When they act it out with me, it's safe.

You have a classic porn star look; blonde hair, huge tits, trim body. We love it! Let's talk about those incredible breasts of yours for a minute.

NE: Why thank you! I'm very proud of my big boobies. They cost a fortune, but thankfully, I get plenty of enjoyment out of them. These are actually my second set of enhanced breasts. Instead of them being 425cc's, these puppies are 650 cc's!

What is your favorite sexual position?

NE: I love the feeling of having a man on top of me, kissing me and fucking me deep. Missionary is the way to go for me. The eye contact is great in that position too.

What makes you wet?

NE: I really love when men speak Spanish to me. I really have a thing for Hispanic men. Also, since I like more aggressive style sex. I love having my hair pulled and my boobs smacked. I also really love kissing and making out.

What kind of music do you enjoy listening to?

NE: I can really get down to some reggae or hip-hop.

We hear you are now on the feature dancing circuit! How is that going for you?

NE: I love feature dancing. It is an awesome way to connect with my fans. It feels more like a traveling circus. I dance for them and try to create a fun experience for all involved. Afterwards, they come up to me, take pictures with me and some even get lap dances. It has been going well, but it does get rather stressful.

Stressful? How so?

NE: I do have a family and am a mother, so my time is very valuable. It's hard for me to take that time off and travel a lot. I try to maintain balance with both my personal and professional life. I enjoy performing in my stage shows. Every town and city has a different crowd full of people, a different vibe and a unique energy.

Which cities have you toured?

NE: I've reached out to Jersey, Philly, New York, and Sacramento, to name a few. Sacramento was great because it is really dear to me. I'm from Northern California and grew up in Modesto. Sacramento was packed, wall-to-wall.

How did that show go?

NE: My roadie told me that the club was not full. It was my first time out, ever, and I was already freaked out. I thought I could test things out with a smaller crowd and get my bearings. He lied! The place was packed, standing room only, wall-to-wall, with people chanting, "Nina! Nina! Nina!" It was my rock star moment and I loved it! They made me feel so warm, fuzzy and welcomed. They were chanting for little ol' me.

Your fan base sounds massive! How exciting!

NE: Yes, you never really know just how large until you see an entire room occupied by people that love and support what you do. The feeling is completely humbling and amazing.

What costumes do you rock on stage?

NE: I love rocking my cop costume. I pack the room full of fog and have sirens blowing. Then, I come out with my aviator sunglasses and shine my flashlight on the crotches of people in the crowd. For people that haven't experienced my shows before, they have a panic attack, assuming that the club is being raided. It's awesome. That show is great fun. I also do a lotion show and let them stick dollar bills to my lotioned up body. The crowd seems to enjoy that show too.

What's the wildest sex you've ever had off camera?

NE: Well, I once sucked my husband's cock while driving down the German Autobahn at 100MPH. How is that for wild? (laughing)

****

Tanya Tate

Birth Date: March 31

Hometown: Liverpool, England

Height: 5'6"

Weight: 126 lbs.

Measurements: 34DD-26-37

Movies:

Big Tit MILFS- Third Degree Films

Beautiful MILF- Daring Media Group

Ass Priming Mommies- Lethal Hardcore

Tanya Tate's Tea & Muffin Party- Filly Films

Tanya Tate- Naughty America

After working in an office setting for several years, what made you decide to try your hand at a career in adult entertainment?

TT: I was really bored working in an office setting and I had just ended a relationship. At the time, I was searching for an exciting new life. Then one evening, I was watching an adult movie with a friend of mine and the idea came to me, 'Hey, I can do that.' I thought about it for a while and then decided that porn was exactly what I wanted to do. From there, I had some really nice pictures taken of myself and researched the internet market and sent those pictures out to production companies. Quickly, I was invited to London where they shot me. This all happened in 2008.

So, it seems as though your life was at a crossroads. We're so glad you had the courage to take a different path.

TT: Yes, thankfully it has worked out extremely well.

Once you affiliated yourself with the industry, was the porn experience all that you expected it to be?

TT: Well, I didn't go into it with too many expectations. I knew it would be different then what you see on the camera. I tried to have an open mind. I just allowed it all to unfold.

Where there any differences or surprises you weren't expecting?

TT: Going on a porn set for the first time was a bit surprising. There were so many new things to see, experience and learn about. In porn, we're learning new things all the time. What seems to be really normal to me now, was so new and foreign to me at the time. I was so nervous in the beginning.

Can you share some details with us regarding your first professional scene?

TT: The first scene that I shot was with a guy named Danny D, who had an eleven-inch cock. That was a surprise! That was a BIG surprise! In fact, a friend of mine and I got out a measuring tape just so we could get the accurate length of it. Yes, he was eleven-inches! He played the role of a handyman that came out to fix my shower. Of course, he ended up cleaning out my pipes instead. It was a hot scene.

Being sexually active with people outside of porn, it isn't likely to run across many that have uncoiling, eleven-inch cocks, is it?

TT: No, it's not likely to run into men with cocks like that. Actually, before I knew what he had in his pants, I was sitting in the make-up chair, getting my hair and make-up done when he came in. Excited for our scene, he began working with himself. When I turned around, his huge cock was in my face. I thought to myself, 'Oh, my God!' It was so funny. (laughing)

Another thing about porn productions that I personally found to be quite surprising was the amount of people it takes to create a single movie.

TT: Yes, but that also depends on the type of set you are on. Some are larger and require more crew than others. For my own website, www.TanyaTate.com, sometimes, it's just me and my cameraman. As my site grew, the crew grew as well, to maybe having a make-up artist and an assistant too. When you shoot for big companies like Digital Playground and Wicked Pictures, the crew is large. There's a person for everything, even a person to help wipe up, a person to hold the camera, a person to hold the mike, a person to hold the script, and so on.

Do you find that you are more comfortable working on a smaller, more intimate set, or a larger, full-scale production?

TT: At this point, it doesn't really matter to me. Whether large or small, it is always a professional environment. I'm fine either way. One time, I shot a movie where a guy actually brought one of his mates along with him on set. When the camera wasn't rolling, his mate was a total jerk and was trying to hit on all the girls, saying stuff like, 'Hey, can I take you out?' That wasn't cool. That wasn't cool at all. This is our place of work. Finally, I had to say something. He was making me feel so uncomfortable. It wasn't cool having this creepy man hitting on everybody while we were trying to make a movie.

Do you think there is a certain misconception that some people may have about you because of what you do for a living?

TT: Oh, yeah! I get it all the time. It's a real turn on to imagine the fans fantasizing about having sex with me at home. In fact, most fans would love to have sex with their favorite porn star. It's when the guys try to turn that fantasy into reality that things get tricky. I do a lot of fan shows and have the privilege of meeting loads of fans. However, some fans can't take no for an answer. Some fans show up and ask to have sex with me or ask me out on a date. If I politely decline, they say, 'Alright then. Fuck you!' or, ' I don't need girls like you. I have lots of girls.' If I say no, other people start complaining and asking why. It makes me feel so uncomfortable. I say to myself, 'Well, I tried my best to be polite.' Just because I am a porn star doesn't meet that I am open to fucking anybody. But, if they insist on fucking me, I tell them to go to www.FuckTanya.com. There, they can purchase my Fleshlight toy, which is an exact replica of my pussy.

What is your preferred time of day to have sex?

TT: It all depends on my mood. Sometimes in the morning, it's fun to get off and start your day by fooling around in the shower. If I've been web-camming all day then my sex drive is going to be high. I'll have to take a break in the middle and take care of business. Really, it all depends on my mood.

If you could fuck anybody on the planet, who would you choose?

TT: What a curious question. Let me think about that one. Actually, I was asked this question once before but I forget what I said. Oh, I remember now. My answer was Sheamus, the Irish wrestler that performs for the WWE. I always tweet about him when he's on the tellie. He's such a big man. I could just imagine him throwing me around the room. How extraordinary!

Of all the porn stars you've worked with, who have you shared the strongest sexual chemistry with?

TT: James Deen is an excellent performer. He puts his all into every one of his scenes. But, the best sexual chemistry is going to come from a guy that is really into me. That is the best feeling and the best scenario. I've also done great scenes with Chris Johnson and Xander Corvus. The industry is full of hot guys. As far as girls are concerned, I adore working with India Summer and Julia Ann. Those women are spectacular. Celeste Star is another girl that is high up on my list, as is Lea Lexis. After my scene with Lea, we couldn't stop kissing each other. I'm spoiled for choice.

What are some of the perks of being an A-List porn star?

TT: Aside from having loads of hot sex? I have developed lots of great friends and am able to reach out to them through Facebook, Twitter, and other social media sites. Even though the relationships are virtual, I've still managed to become really good friends with people from around the world. That means a lot to me. Since my fans know I love comic books, they often send me great copies of comics or statues of my favorite characters. The presents are really sweet and appreciated. If fans send me lingerie, I take pictures of myself in it and send it to them. My position in porn makes me feel happy and very grateful.

What are some of your guilty pleasures?

TT: I love white chocolate cookies. They are so delicious. I heat them up in the microwave and eat them with vanilla ice cream. I also enjoy eating cupcakes. I wish that sweets weren't so bad for you. After eating those types of goodies, I really need to work out even harder at the gym.

As one of the most beloved and respected MILF/Cougar performers in the industry today, what do you think it is about this category of women that drives men wild?

TT: The idea of bedding a hot, experienced, older woman, who knows what she wants is an unbeatable combination. This type of woman is in total control of her sexuality. Sometimes, I suppose, some men would want that type of woman to take control over them too. I have a lot of fans that request fantasy role-playing where they'd like me to play the role of a hot mum. These guys want to be seduced by me. It's the image of a hotter, older woman who is out there getting what she wants, how she wants it, that drives men crazy.

What do you consider your sexiest physical attribute?

TT: Many fans have commented on my boobs, my legs and my feet. I keep my feet and hands up and have a pedicure and a manicure done every two weeks. I'm always dolled up from head to toe. My fans love to see me in stockings, showing off my long legs. Can I pick all three?

In your professional life, do you enjoy working with the younger talent, or do you prefer fucking the seasoned players?

TT: Again, it depends on my mood. Sometimes it's nice to feel like a kid in a candy shop with so many yummy possibilities to choose from. The seasoned players certainly know what to do, so you know you are going to get off and have a great time. As far as the newbies are concerned, sometimes it's fun being more aggressive with them and teaching them how things are done. It's fun manipulating the scene with the newbies, in conjunction with the director, of course, and telling them what to do. They just look at me with their bright eyes and say, 'Okay, Tanya.'

Are you the type of person that likes to dominate, or be dominated?

TT: I'm not really a submissive person. But, if I'm working with a performer like James Deen, I just know I'm going to be thrown around everywhere. With him, there's no choice. He's fantastic!

Are you a practicing cougar on and off camera?

TT: (laughing) I bet they all want to know that, don't they? I'll have to say that I think that younger men certainly have a lot of sexual stamina and they can just go, go, go. They are definitely a lot of fun. I've enjoyed many. We'll just leave it at that. (laughing)

Are you known for bringing your work home with you?

TT: This sounds like another question coming directly from the mouth of a fan, is it?

Yes, it is! Enquiring minds want to know the ins and outs of the great, Tanya Tate.

TT: (laughing) Since I web cam at home, I will say, 'Yes!'

Do you have any special talents?

TT: Well, I am really good at dirty talking. I love dirty talking to the camera, with my sexy accent. Men love my accent. And, I used to drive a motor bike. I would ride it around and it was hot having so much power beneath my legs. Since I wasn't riding it around as much as I would have liked to, I sold it and bought myself a pair of boobs instead. I think my fans would all agree that I made a great choice!

****

18437937R00051

Printed in Great Britain
by Amazon